The Last Herd

A season in the working life of the Royal Parks' and Historic Royal Palaces' Shires, the last working Shire herd in London.

By

Paul Stewart.

With a foreword by
H.R.H. The Prince of Wales.

Photography into ART

The Last Herd

First published in the UK in 2017

by Photography Into ART

9 Tree Close
Petersham
Surrey
TW10 7BA
United Kingdom

www.photographyintoart.co.uk

A CIP catalogue record for this book is available from the British Library.

ISBN 978-0-9957092-1-8

Thanks to:-

H.R.H. The Prince of Wales, Dr. Andreas Liefooghe, Edward MacDowell, Tom Nixon, Tanya Melton, Rebecca Law, Jason Debney, Linda Duffield, Katie Rawll, Sergio Salvagio, Joe Gadd, Monica Brimacombe and all the volunteers who are seen working with the Shires in this book and those behind the scenes. All the staff of the Royal Parks and Historic Royal Palaces and of course the The Royal Parks OCU of the Metropolitan Police. John Ingham of the Daily Express, and indeed all my colleagues at the Express who have put up with me banging on about Shire horses for a year or more. Epson UK, Seawhites of Brighton, Domke camera bags and all the others who helped with this book and the exhibition.

Not forgetting Aragon, Roy, Heath, Nobby, Joey, Tom, Massey and Murdoch, "The Last Herd".

Special thanks to Mr. Luke Herbert, without whom this and other projects would not have been possible. My family and most especially and always my wife Vivien, to whom this book is dedicated...

Contents

4

Foreword by H.R.H. The Prince of Wales

CLARENCE HOUSE

Nearly 500 years ago, King Henry VIII started the process of developing the ultimate warhorse. In 1535 he introduced The Breed of Horses Act to halt a marked decline in the quality and size of horses. The King is credited with giving the resulting large and powerful breed of horses the name Shire – from the Saxon word *schyran*. This means to shear or divide, and gives us the word 'shire' as a synonym for 'county.'

This remarkable breeding programme persisted for more than three centuries, during which time the original large warhorse had transformed into the great agricultural workhorse that met so many of the demands of the Industrial Revolution. In the 1890s, there were estimated to be around a million Shire horses in the country, but the internal combustion engine proved to be even more powerful and after the Second World War the breed became all but redundant and virtually died out. Today, Shire horses are designated at risk by the Rare Breeds Survival Trust, of which I have been proud to be Patron for the past thirty years in an increasingly desperate attempt to help preserve our unique native herds of farm animals and birds. In London, where once the brewing trade alone employed more than six thousand of these extraordinary horses, only one working herd remains.

Operation Centaur's mission is to ensure that the eight working Shires in their care continue to adapt and remain firmly in the public eye. To this end, the photojournalist, Paul Stewart, followed the herd for over a year and has produced a remarkable record, beautifully told, of its activities throughout the seasons.

"The Last Herd" considers the contemporary relevance of working horses in the most urban situations. It is clear that the Shire horse, while unable to compete with heavy machinery in open countryside, can more than hold its own in the smaller woodlands, parks and wildflower meadows that are such a special feature of London, and it does so in a way that has minimal detrimental impact on these sensitive eco-systems. In partnership with The Royal Parks and Historic Royal Palaces, Operation Centaur's Shires work skilfully with their handlers and are a sight to behold, lifting the spirits of everyone fortunate enough to see them in action. I had the opportunity to see their work myself during the sowing of the 90th new Coronation Meadow in The Green Park, dedicated to Her Majesty The Queen.

In a further extension of their role, Operation Centaur now deploys its Shires as co-therapists in equine-assisted psychotherapy and learning. Shires that log trees and mow hay are also helping schools deal with bullying, raising the self-esteem of women prisoners and teaching that strength lies in collaboration, while leadership potential resides in us all. Words cannot do justice to what people experience when they find themselves face to face with a huge horse that weighs over a ton...

It is perhaps this numinous quality in the Shire horse that speaks to our collective imagination – a very British symbol of strength and gentleness, power and grace. It is rooted in the past, relevant today, and has a unique role to play in whatever the future may hold. The story of the Shire is not just one of horses; it is about our traditional skills, our heritage and what we choose to conserve for the benefit of future generations.

Introduction

I learned to ride when I was young and I've trekked on horses (not to mention camels and an elephant) on five continents, although I'll admit I've done a lot more by 4x4. So I've long liked horses and big animals and a few years ago, I was sad to hear that the last of the working Shire horses from the breweries had left London. In fact, I didn't think there were any working Shire horses left in the capital at all. However, shortly after moving to Petersham in Richmond, I was driving through Richmond Park when I saw a pair of magnificent Shires, mowing the verges at the side of the road. Shortly thereafter, while researching a completely different project, I met with Tom Nixon of Operation Centaur in Kew Gardens. He put me in contact with Dr Andreas Liefooghe and I went to meet him at King George's Old Hunting Lodge in Richmond Park. Holly Lodge is one of the bases of Operation Centaur. This charity does all manner of work with various horses including operating the Royal Parks' Shires, though I was soon to find out, they were the last working herd, at that time, of 7, now happily of 8 working Shires in the capital.

When I first met Andreas, he was taking Murdoch out to graze in a pasture, almost hand feeding him as the horse had just had a major operation to remove over 20 feet of his intestines due to a twisted gut. Murdoch was, as you can imagine, looking pretty sorry for himself and it was the care and attention that Andreas was giving him that led me to understand that these were terrific people and made me want to document their care of the horses. In fact I was out on that day, shooting on black & white film for another project, and the image of Andreas and Richard taking Murdoch from the stable is the first image of over two and a half thousand shot for the "Last Herd" project.

LAST OF THE SHIRE HORSES

Shire horses at Buck Hill.

A feature in the Daily Express generated from the "Last Herd" Project.

A century ago there were one million of them in Britain, today only one working stable is left in London and fewer than 1,500 worldwide

By Jane Warren

THEY were once a familiar sight in every town and village in this country, pulling drays and working the land. But as mechanisation took over, the shire horse population has gone into near-terminal decline.

"There were a million of these horses 100 years ago in England at the beginning of the First World War," says Ed Marlhewell, who works as a coachman with London's last surviving stable of seven shire horses. "And now, worldwide, there are fewer than 1,500."

This means these gentle equine tractors are rarer than the giant panda, of which there are believed to be around 1,800 worldwide. The UK Rare Breeds Survival Trust considers the shire horse breed to be "at risk".

At the turn of the last century there were 40,000 shire horses in London alone. "Now London has just one herd of these magnificent beasts, the seven working horses of the royal parks and historic royal palaces," says Daily Express photographer Paul Stewart who is working on a project to record a year in the life of these majestic creatures.

This will lead to a photographic exhibition and a book to raise money for Operation Centaur, the organisation that looks after them.

"Originally bred at Hampton Court at the command of King Henry VIII as a large horse to carry fully armoured knights into battle, the horses are used for all manner of tasks, including mowing and logging," he adds.

And it is these traditional agricultural pursuits Paul is cataloguing, alongside their ceremonial role at Hampton Court and Richmond Park, which includes offering carriage rides to visitors.

"From the early morning grooming in their old Home Farm stables at 7.30am and out to Hampton Court to pull a two-ear tram for the tourists, it is fantastic to see how everyone loves these gentle giants," says Paul, who is frequently to be found near the stables, camera in hand, in the early morning mists of west London.

But there the connection with the past stops. For the managing director of Operation Centaur has created a brave new future for the shire horse in which the animals are also being used in innovative ways.

For the past 25 years Dr Andreas Liefooghe's training as a psychotherapist has also seen him using the animals in his counselling practice.

Among other projects, his shire horses have partnered with charities working with children being bullied and people with autism.

"There is no magic involved in equine assisted psychotherapy, it is about getting people to work in groups with horses and learn from how the horse relates," says the lifelong horseman, who describes his role at the helm of Operation Centaur as his dream job. "Horses don't know if someone is a chief executive or a PA, instead they respond to the energy that people bring."

And his approach also informs the way in which the animals carry out their agricultural role when they are contracted by local authorities in London, as well as by the royal parks and historic palaces.

"This country would not have been built were it not for the shire horse," says Dr Liefooghe. "They were the lorries of their day and they had a very functional role. The industrial revolution couldn't have started if shire horses had not been working on the docks. They were the white vans of industrial revolution and they were as ubiquitous.

"People think they were agricultural but shires were also in cities and towns, they were everywhere."

He is determined to show that shire horses can be just as relevant today. "We are trying to go beyond this nostalgic romanticised image of the past. Yes, they have an important heritage but in the pockets of green we still have – and remember London is 50 per cent green – they can be used in places where we wouldn't want heavy machinery to come in."

The big enemy of a wildflower meadow is ground compaction. "If you use heavy machinery you are destroying the under-soil where shire horses are not only very popular but very nimble, they also have a low carbon footprint," says Dr Liefooghe.

HE CLAIMS that every single civic task that is currently done with machinery can be done with shire horses, including the removal of rubbish, the collection of recycling, road sweeping, watering the plants and planting. "Everything a borough now does on a daily basis," he insists. In Petersham, Surrey, the verges are being cut by shire horses and the lawns at Kensington Palace are cut with a horse-drawn mower.

Dr Liefooghe is also richly persuasive about the additional benefits to the local community when imaginative councils contract out these functions to real horse power.

"What normally happens is that to cut costs everything councils do is being subcontracted but their management planning is removed from any natural cycles and from any sense of community that inhabit those places.

"We can't compete on price and convenience – you have to look after horses and feed them and they work more slowly than machinery – but when we do a job we always go in and get the local community involved. They are mobilised rather than alienated. It is old-fashioned stewardship of the land rather than the fragmented, outsourced way things are done today."

The animals were originally bred for equally practical reasons at Hampton Court. It was there that Henry VIII began his breeding programme to produce the largest horses in the world – the antecedents of these remaining beasts.

He envisaged a great war horse capable of carrying a knight in full armour after he was dismayed by the puny horses that were prevalent in England at the time.

BUT the increasing role of gunpowder eventually brought an end to their use in battle: Oliver Cromwell's cavalry favoured lighter, faster mounts and the bigger breed began to be used for draught work instead.

The breed, which stands more than 16 hands high (5ft 4in) at the withers has an enormous capacity for weight pulling and throughout its history has been popular for hauling brewery wagons delivering ale to customers.

It was 10 years ago this month that the famous Yorkshire brewery Tetley's stopped using the powerful horses to pull their drays after the company was taken over by Danish brewer Carlsberg and their upkeep was considered too expensive.

However there are many environmental reasons why the use of heavy horses is preferable to using machinery on the land.

"You want the least amount of impact out there and horses offer that," says MacDowell at the Hampton Court Palace stables. "You can't find us if we're working out there because we don't make any noise. It's not like you've got a chainsaw or a strimmer.

"You can't keep these horses as pets, they eat too much. A horse like that will eat a dustbin full of feed plus hay so they have to have a job. And they're happier working. I never get fed up of talking about them. They are my babies really."

● For more information see www.operationcentaur.com

PULLING POWER: Aragon and Royal, two of the shire horses of the last working herd in London, mowing the spring grass in Hyde Park, driven by Ed McDowell. Top right: Massey and Heath draw the passenger tram at Hampton Court Palace. Top left: Putting in a shift at Tetley's Brewery in Leeds, 1966

As a press photographer, I am lucky to get more than a few minutes to work with a subject. Even in depth photojournalistic projects I have undertaken in the past have rarely lasted more than 3 or 4 weeks, so to have a whole year to document a working season was both a luxury and a fairly daunting challenge. However, I did see that as well as a book, this would be great for the paper and it soon produced some great features, which in turn generated publicity for the work of the Royal Parks' and Palaces' Shires and Operation Centaur. From my point of view, I think it's worked incredibly well. I hope you agree.

Paul Stewart

Petersham

England

June 2017

Shire Horses, A Brief History - and an eye to the future.....

So What is a Shire Horse? A Short History.

For many years the Shire horse was the backbone of British Agriculture and Industry. For almost 500 years, until the coming of the steam and internal combustion engines, these magnificent animals provided the best motive power available. However, their route was not as an agricultural animal. Nearly 500 years ago, Henry VIII felt the need to breed the ultimate war horse, the best available, and he instituted two Acts of Parliament to rigorously control the breeding of horses in England and only allow beasts of exceptional stature to breed. This breeding programme went on as late as the 19th century when the Acts were repealed. Henry VIII is further credited the naming of this powerful new breed of horse, Shire, from the Saxon word Schyran. This means to shear or divide from where we get the name Shire as in county. The Shire Horse became and still is the largest horse in the world. They can stand as tall as 20 hands (nearly 7 foot) at the withers in comparison to the average race horse, which is 16 hands.

Most people credit the invention of the steam engine as the start of the industrial revolution. As true as this may be, it could not have happened without the working horses of the day. It's all well and good to build a steam engine at the head of one's mine or in a factory, but unless the mine is a coal mine, how do you get the coal to the steam engine in the first place? The answer, as ever, was the trusty horse, with Shires being particularly suitable in this role. Once it was discovered that a horse could move 50 times more weight on water than it could on roads at the time, canals quickly became popular and a network was established throughout the country with adjacent tow paths so that the narrow boats, loaded with goods, could be pulled up and down the length and breadth of these islands.

In 1893 in his book "The Horse World of London", W.J. Gordon noted that there were over 6,000 Shires employed in the brewery trade alone. A further 1,100 were owned by the Great Western Railway to carry goods to and from trains arriving at the London termini. Indeed, one of their stables had 4 floors of horses on an industrial scale.   He also noted that these horses were well cared for, their collars, for instance, going into a drying room overnight so that, "in the morning they could be put on as warm and snug as a pair of socks". Shires pulled buses and later trams and were responsible for moving a huge amount of goods around the City. In fact, they were even responsible for removing one and a half million tons per year of refuse away from the City. Industrial London could never have developed without them. They formed a goodly part of London's commerce with at least two sale yards being dedicated to the sale of "Draft Horses". A number of commentators have estimated that the number of Shires in the UK at that time was around a million and Gordon estimated that at that time there were 30 to 40,000 in London alone. In fact, 1893 saw over 6000 Shire horses being used in the Brewery trade in London alone and more were used by distillers and vintners. This association with alcoholic beverages may explain part of the popularity of these gentle giants.

In the late 20th century, Whitbread and other breweries were still using their horses to deliver, but these days, there are none left in London and those that still belong to brewers, such as the Fullers' Shires at Windlesham, are mainly used for shows. Today we have one last working herd of eight Shires - this is their story.

The 1980's black and white images in this section are of the Whitbread Shires and Tetley Shires. Pictures by Hilaria McCarthy, reproduced courtesy of Express Newspapers.

A number of environmental experts, see "Horse Power" as a positive force. Here John Ingham, the Environment Editor of the Daily Express, gives us his take on the Shires.

Shire horses are helping to reinvent the wheel when it comes to managing the Royal Parks in an environmentally friendly manner. These wonderful workhorses are taking the parks back to the future by working the land in a traditional way to protect fauna and flora for generations yet to come. At the same time they are greener when it comes to the curse of pollution. They are much quieter than modern machines which causes less disruption to wildlife, and they have a much lower carbon footprint than engines powered by fossil fuels, these nimble animals can reach the parts of the park machines cannot - particularly steep slopes.

The Shires are used for a wide range of tasks from mowing the grasslands to forestry, from controlling bracken to managing reed beds. With every sedate step they are lighter than, say, tractors, so they compact the soil less which is good news for wild flowers. The slow pace of the horses also allows their human helpers to avoid ground-nesting birds in a way that machines sometimes cannot. In Richmond Park the Shires are helping to restore the largest area of lowland acid grassland habitat in Greater London. This area is important for wildlife, birds and insects which all specialise in life on poorer soil. In the past a lot of this grassland was "improved" with fertilisers to make it better for grazing. So hay is grown to reduce the soil fertility and allow the acid grassland to return. The Shires' role is to pull a horse-drawn hay cutter, with the dried grass used as fodder or compost for use elsewhere in the park.

Another threat to the acid grassland is the rampant spread of bracken. The best way found to control these ferns is "bracken-bashing". The Shires pull special bracken rollers that bruise the stems of the ferns. This in turn forces the bracken to use the energy stored in its underground roots to repair itself instead of spreading

even further across the grass. In the winter the Shires return, towing a harrow to aerate the soil and remove dead vegetation. The horses are also a key player in woodland management, able to reach the less accessible areas while avoiding saplings. Reed beds, vital habitat for wildlife from warblers to otters, are also easier to manage with horses than heavy machinery. When trees have been felled, reed beds and hay harvested, the horses take it all away on flatbed drays - just as they did for centuries before the invention of tractors. But there is another advantage to working with these majestic beasts. Shire horses are "at risk" according to the rare Breeds watch-list. By earning their keep, these powerful horses which have worked so well and so closely for so long with man can avoid going the way of the Dodo, now that has got to be a bonus for all of us.

Pictures - Previous page - Tom and Andy logging in Richmond Park with Nobby and Murdoch. This page Tom and Edward mow the park verges with Roy and Aragon.

A Meadow in the West End
Buck Hill,
Kensington Gardens.

Buck Hill - The meadow project - Our year begins.

A spring day marks the start of "The Last Herd" project, a year in the working life of the Royal Parks' and Historic Royal Palaces' Shires. Buck Hill in Kensington Gardens is an area between Hyde Park and Kensington Palace. The space has been created as a meadow and there is a three year trial to see how cultivating with horses will affect the way the pasture regenerates itself.

As the horses do not compact the soil, being much lighter than tractors, the effect on the germination of old seeds lying dormant in the soil is marked. Some species of wild flower, which hadn't been seen in the parks for 80 years, are thriving in this environment and kestrels have been seen there for the first time in years.

During May, working with volunteers, Roy and Aragon were taken to Buck Hill to give the meadow its first cut of the year using their old reciprocating mower. Ed, Tom and Tanya cut the grass enabling the volunteers to gather it together in windrows so it could later be taken off and used.

Pictures -

Opposite page - Edward at the top of Buck Hill preparing to drive Roy and Aragon pulling the reciprocating mower.

Page 20 and 21 - The team work with the volunteers to cut and clear the Buck Hill meadow.

Pictures -

This page - Tom adjusts and clears the mower for a better cut.

Page 23 - The team continue with the harvesting, the vista of Kensington Palace Gardens, The Long Water and the Henry Moore statue behind them.

Pictures -

Left - Roy and Aragon have a rest at the end of the work session.

Right - Tom, Edward and Tanya at the end of the days work.

The Last Herd

The Tourist Trade-1,
The Hampton Court Tram

Hampton Court - The Tram.

Spring sees the start of regular rides for tourists at Hampton Court Palace, one of the most famous Historic Royal Palaces in the world. Hampton Court dates back to Tudor times and the building, its contents and the gardens are world renowned. Hampton Court is also the spiritual home of the Shire horse, so what better way to see round the gardens than being pulled in the tram by Massey and Heath. Not only is this the best way to see the gardens but the Shires themselves are an attraction with tourists lining up to photograph them and be photographed with them.

The Operation Centaur team also give a great guided tour as the vehicle makes its way round the ewe tree lined walkways. But if you are going to take tourists round a Royal Palace or a Royal Park, you have to be really well turned out, so Ed and Tom (with a little help from Andreas) spend a long time grooming the horses before fitting their beautifully polished tack. They then change into their own finery and walk the horses from the old 17th century stable, which in itself was preceded by a line of stables on the same site where the original English War Horse was bred, over to the tram where it is hooked up so they can go off to meet today's travellers.

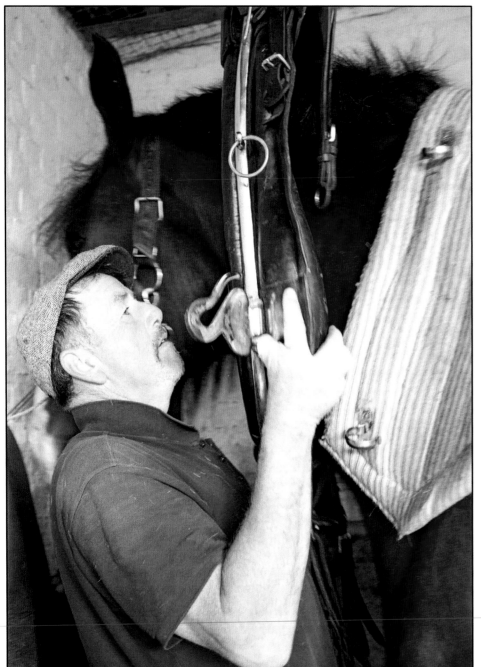

Pictures -

Page 28/29 - Tom with a little help from Andreas gets Heath ready for work on the Tram.

Left - Tom puts Massey's collar on.

Below - a detail of part of a harness used by the Royal Parks' Shires. This and the collars are designed so the horses can pull their loads comfortably.

Right - Edward and Tom take Massey and Heath from the stables to Hampton Court Palace to pull the Tram.

Edward and Tom connect the Shires' harness to the tram and then they move off to meet the visitors. The Shires are hugely popular and give many rides throughout the season. They are also very popular with serious photographers and those who just snap images on their mobile phones.

"Wow Dad, look at them...... Are they real?"

Many younger visitors are enthralled by the horses, as in these days of cable and satellite TV, video games and the internet, their chance to see and interact with living creatures is limited. This prompted one young lad to turn to his father and say, "Wow dad, look at them...... Are they real?"

As Hampton Court Palace is the spiritual home of the Shire horse, it's apt that they carry the tourists round and the team give an interesting running commentary, imparting information about the Palace and it's history.

34

Pictures:-

Page 32 - Edward checks Heath's bridle and bit as he and Tom connect the harness to the Tram.

Page 33 - Tom checks the Tram as Ed drives it to the front of the palace to pick up passengers.

Far left, left and above - Visitors love to photograph the Shires when they see them.

Page 36/37 - The Tram takes tourists round the Historic Gardens. Edward collects fares from visitors Christine and Metin.

The Last Herd

The Tourist Trade-2, The New Park Brake

The New Park Brake.

In April, Operation Centaur got a new vehicle to be used with the Shires in Richmond Park. This is an eight seat "brake". A brake is a horse-drawn carriage used originally in the 19th and early 20th centuries in the training of horses for draft work. It was a sturdy chassis used to "break" a horse. The term was then applied to the shooting-brake, which was a carriage used to carry beaters, gamekeepers and sportsmen with their dogs, guns and game.

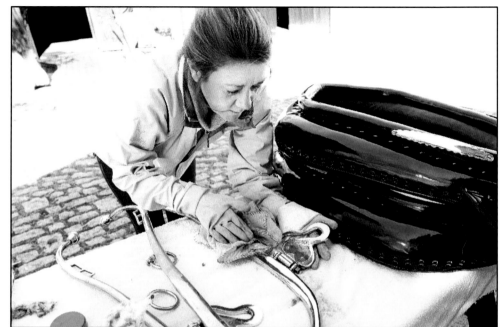

Then came purpose built shooting-brakes designed to carry the driver and a footman or gamekeeper at the front, facing forward, and passengers on longitudinal benches with their dogs, guns and game. As Richmond Park was originally a royal hunting ground, it's a very appropriate type of carriage to use for visitors to the park. The new brake takes a total of eight people so six passengers at a time can have a fantastic ride, which in turn enables more conservation work with the horses.

Before the new vehicle could be used for the highly popular rides, it needed to be thoroughly checked out and photographed to launch it. This resulted in much cleaning and polishing of tack, harnesses etc. and

40

the grooming and preparation of Roy and Aragon, the two oldest and most experienced of the Royal Parks' Shires. Tanya Melton working with volunteer and Operation Centaur horse sharer, Katie Rawll, polished leather and metal till it glowed and Tom and Edward made sure the Shires were well turned out. They were then coupled up to the brake and went round the route they use to take visitors on the 60 minute off the beaten track ride that passes White Lodge, now the home of the Royal Ballet School. They stopped in many locations for photography, which has been used to promote the rides. As all who go on these rides agree there is no better way to see the park and its many inhabitants such as the Red and Fallow deer.

Pictures -

Page 40 - Katie Rawll polishes tack to get it perfect for the photo shoot.

Page 41 - Tanya Melton checks the harness.

Page 42 - Getting the Shires ready and a fallow deer looks on as the horses pass.

Page 43 - Edward drives the brake past White Lodge with Tanya Melton.

Page 44 - Top - Turning into Queen's Ride.

Below - Fallow Deer near Pembroke Lodge.

Opposite page - The team on Queen's Ride, with White Lodge in the distance.

The Last Herd

The Park Keepers

Richmond Park is the largest of the Royal Parks in London. It's unique acid grassland needs looking after and the Royal Parks' Shires play a major role in this care. From one of their two bases, Holly Lodge, (the other is at Home Farm in Hampton Court Palace), they carry out many different roles, one of the most public being mowing the roadside verges. It's not uncommon to see visitors showing sheer delight at the sight of two horses pulling the mower along the side of the road. Within a day of the mowing, new sweet shoots emerge and these are a real favourite of the Park's Red and Fallow deer.

One problem is bracken, if left unchecked, it can rapidly grow to encompass all of the grass. However, it is also necessary to provide cover and nesting habitat for the rich diversity of wildlife that make Richmond Park so special. Everything from foxes to skylarks need the bracken, so the problem is one of balance. The solution is to use special "Bracken Bashing" rollers. These bruise and crack the stems of the plants and the plants efforts go into repairing the damage rather than spreading.

So, in the park, the summer months are taken up with managing the grassland and taking tourists on rides round the park, making this one of the busiest times for "The Last Herd".

Pictures -

Page 48 and 49 - Preparing Roy and Aragon to mow the verges in Richmond Park.

Page 50 - A close up of the mower, mowing on Sawyers Hill and a close up of the Royal Parks' insignia on Roy's harness.

Page 51 - Mowing the verge on Sawyers Hill, the whole of London stretched out behind.

Page 52 - Tom Nixon with Murdoch, "Bracken Bashing" by Holly Lodge.

Page 53 - Tanya Melton with Heath and Tom "Bracken Bashing" between Kidney and Sidmouth Woods.

This page - a close up of the the special "Bracken Bashing" roller.

Opposite page - Tanya Melton with Heath and Tom "Bracken Bashing" between Kidney Wood and Sidmouth Wood.

54

Pictures -

Pages 56 to 59 - After a hard days work, we all like to come home to a shower, bath or even a shampoo and set and the equine staff are no exception. Back at Holly Lodge, Tom spends quite a time washing and grooming Roy and Aragon before they are dried, covered and stabled for the night.

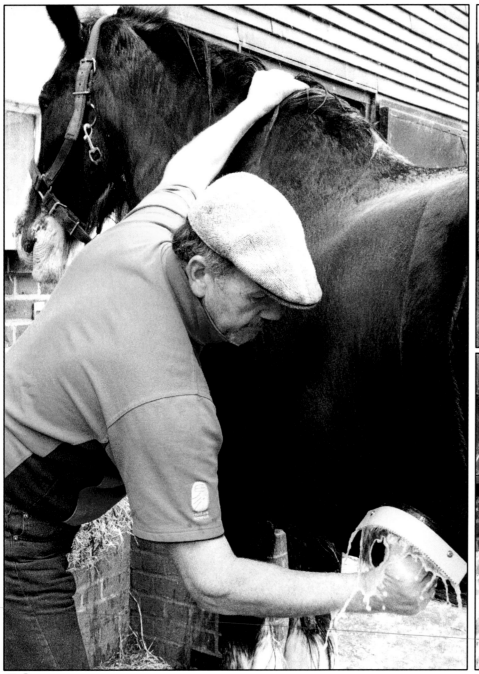

The Last Herd

The Farrier's Tale

The Farrier's Tale - They Shoe Horses Don't They...

Horses hooves need constant attention and a shod horse will need shoes changing, even if they're not worn out. The reason is that, like human nails, the hoof is growing constantly and the metal shoe, while protecting the foot, prevents the hoof from wearing away so the hoof will need trimming from under the metal shoe.

Luckily, Operation Centaur have Head Coachman Edward MacDowell, a qualified farrier who holds a DipFWF, a diploma from the Worshipful Company of Farriers, one of the city trade guilds that has been responsible for the training and certification of farriers since about 1356, though these records were largely lost in the Great Fire of London in 1666. The first charter of the modern WCF dates from 1674. Edward has been a farrier for almost 50 years and this is evident in the skilful way he works with all the horses in his care.

The shoes are heated in a furnace, often gas powered these days rather than the old style coal hearth used by blacksmiths and farriers of old. Once the shoe is heated the farrier uses his skills to shape it to the horses hoof, it's then fitted hot, to make it seat properly, which as the hoof is made of keratin like human nails, makes it a painless process. The shoe is then nailed on, as they have been for thousands of years, to protect the delicate parts of the horse's foot.

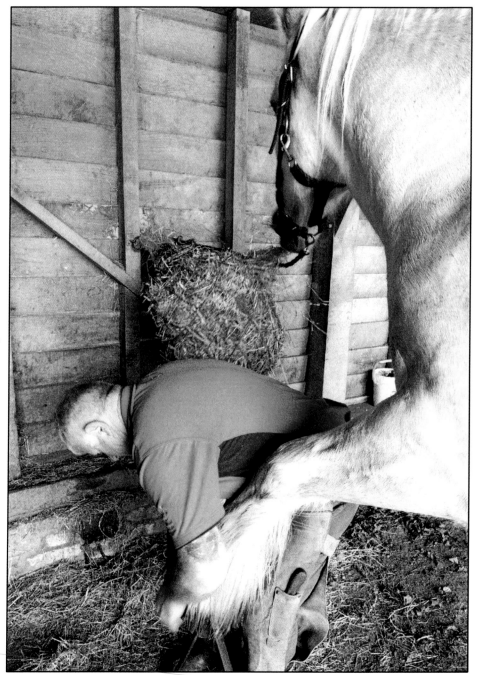

62

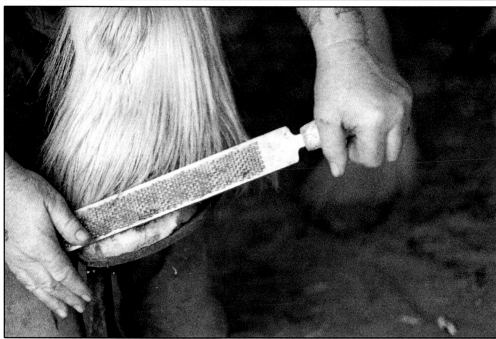

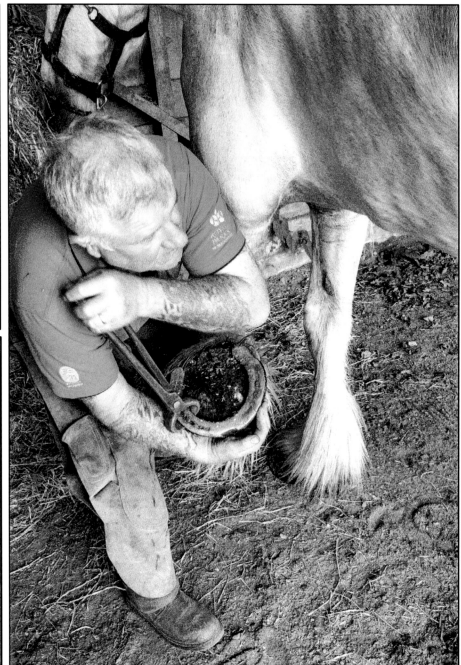

Pictures -

Page 62 - Heath places his hoof on the stand so Edward can prepare it.

Page 63 - clockwise from the top - The red hot shoe is shaped to fit, the old shoe is removed and after the new shoe is fitted, the hoof is filed.

This page - below some old worn shoes ready for recycling.

Right - Edward and Heath are joined by Tom Nixon after the shoeing is complete.

Opposite page - the red hot shoe is painlessly burned in to the keratin hoof for a perfect fit.

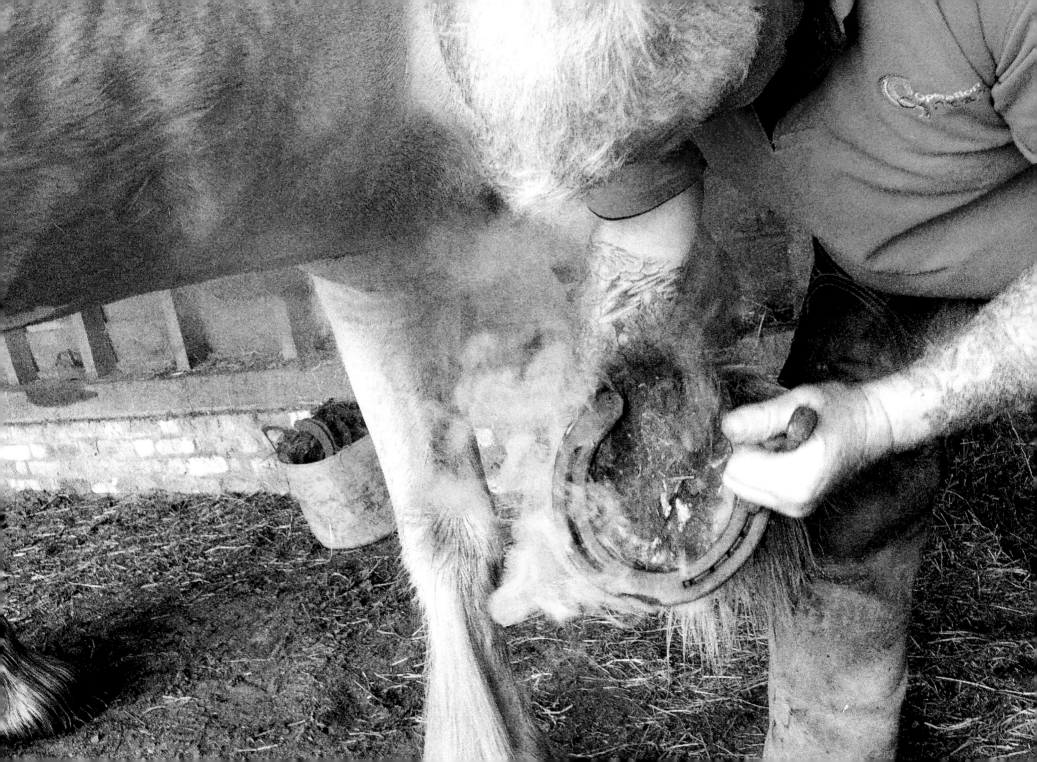

The Last Herd

Four Legged Environmentalists

Four Legged Environmentalists and the Thames Landscape Strategy - A talk with Jason Debney and Rebecca Law of TLS.

Thames Landscape Strategy is a hundred year vision for the Arcadian Thames Corridor between Hampton and Kew and it is a partnership organisation that brings together 14 funding agencies with 280 community groups to enhance, conserve and manage this wonderful river landscape and part of the project work that we do is restoration. About 10 years ago, Thames Landscape Strategy got a Heritage Lottery Fund bid to restore the complex of avenues at Ham which are recognised as the most important 17th century avenues in Europe and they were very decayed, completely overgrown and in a desperate need of restoration. Over a period of 10 years, we have slowly restored the Avenues back to their former glory. Once the Avenues were restored, the way that the Thames Landscape Strategy works, because it is a hundred year plan is that we don't just sit back and let them grow over again, which happens so often with restoration work, we actively go out there and manage it, to keep the standard of the Avenues up. So working with Operation Centaur is a way of managing the Avenues so we can keep the high standard of the restoration going for the next decade.

Horses are a lot more sensitive to the landscape - you don't have tyre tracks, you don't have heavy machinery. You can take small mowers down onto the Avenues, but because they are so long, the contractors do tend to either use a larger machine to get it done fast or they were using the smaller machines but still trying to get it done as quickly as possible rather than necessarily doing it in keeping with the rest of the project. So what we thought would be a much better idea was to have volunteers working to keep the scrub down. Obviously once the vegetation overgrows, you can't mow the ground any more because there are brambles and so on in the way so even machines struggle and there isn't the capacity to do that as part of the normal mowing processes - it is a unique environment.

So horses were chosen because they are a lot more sensitive, they don't damage the ground, so that even if it is wet weather, you don't have the same amount of track and travel up and down. They only leave footprints, they don't leave oil stains or petrol fumes - occasionally a bit of manure but that's good for the grass and good for the wild flowers and the other reason for using them, particularly on this set of avenues is because they are 17th century landscape, it's in keeping with how they would have been managed - not exactly how they would have been

managed but in the 17th century you would have seen work horses and labour staff doing this this type of work, which is why it has been such a good partnership with the National Trust, who now manage the actual property. The landscape however is managed by the council, so it sort of helps everybody achieve the same goal and everybody loves coming out and seeing the horses out there doing it.

There is also the historic element of this as well as horses being much more in keeping with the way that the Avenues would have been managed in the 17th century. The cut that you get - the finish - from horses, looks like the cut you would have had in the 17th century. If you cut it with a tractor or a lawn mower, you get a very short, fine cut and that is a very modern thing. That cuts type of managed clipped grass only came about in probably the Edwardian times with the invention of the lawn mower, whereas before grass was a lot longer because either a horse would have mown it or you would have had gangs of servants coming out from Ham House with scythes and sickles and everyone from even some of the minor aristocracy at hay making time were out making hay, to get it done before it got wet because it was such an important crop, so we can get a much more historically correct finish to it. It also has huge benefits for the ecology of the

Pictures - Page 68/69 - Edward and Tanya cutting the cow parsley on Petersham Avenue and a close up of the reciprocating cutter. Edward drives Heath and Tom pulling the rotary mower on the Great South Avenue with Tom and Tanya. Ham House is behind them.

Page 70/71 - Roy and Aragon on Petersham Avenue, Tom Nixon helps turn Roy and Aragon by the old Gate House.

Above - Local MP Zac Goldsmith meets the horses, the team and the TLS Volunteers, mowing on Petersham Lane.

Page 73 - The team turn round by Ham Polo Club.

Page 75 - TLS volunteers load the hay on to the dray. Great South Avenue, Ham.

area because by cutting it and raking the grass off, it means we move a lot of the goodness from the area and the nutrients and it means that over the years we hope to see many more wild flowers coming in to the Avenues as well.

We are hoping to work with Operation Centaur on a lot of other projects and take them beyond just working on the Avenues. We have already started having them do some stuff on the Riverside, doing some of the management along the tow path and where they can and they have been doing some work on the Home Park project which was our water meadows restoration at Home Park, which is the other stables for the Shire team, so we have had them where they have learned to do some logging with one of the contractors up there and they were doing felling and then the horses were being used to move the material around the site, again, meaning we didn't have to get vehicles into there and they are also doing the management or working with the Historical Royal Palaces' staff on the management of the reed bed on the bottom of their fields and we restored the reed bed but it needs constant maintenance. When the horses cut it, as they can use their side cutter, like they do on the long grass, it all falls intact and therefore can be bundled. The long term aim of that is to have a useable thatch.

There's a good PR and community relations value in having the Shires on a project, it gets us volunteers, it gets us press, it gets more people out because even if they don't really know what the project is, they want to see the horses and then they ask why the horses are there and there's our cue in for the actual project. There's also a very practical economic reason for using horses at Ham Avenues, for example, the money to fund the horses cutting Ham Avenues was funded by Petersham Environment Trust. The money that we have in the public purse is reduced year on year and the management of Parks and Gardens is non statutory, so they don't have to do it, so the money is drying up and so we have to find exciting and very innovative ways to pay for it. You try persuading local people, local trusts to pay for a tractor to mow it - they will not give you the money but mention horses pulling a mower, that sort of thing, they will pay for it because it is something different. So that's a very good economic argument for using them as well.

The Last Herd

The Royal Visit

The 90th Coronation Meadow

The Green Park

The Coronation Meadow - The Green Park

In September we had the sowing of the 90th Coronation Meadow, dedicated to H.M.The Queen, in The Green Park. Prince Charles took part in the sowing with some school children. The Shires were responsible for a large part of the harrowing and Roy and Aragon were well turned out for the event.

Some of the wildflower seed ended up in a Royal turn up and despite shaking the leg, some will have made it back to Clarence House.

H.R.H. was extremely interested in the Shires and talked and shared a laugh with the team. The world's press were there and Royal correspondents Richard Palmer of the Express and Valentine Low of the Times wasted no time in finding out what he said, from the horses mouth.

78

80

The Last Herd

Therapists (Really)

Equine Assisted Psychotherapy

An unexpected new role for the Shires is Equine Assisted Psycotherapy. Operation Centaur's Dr. Andreas Liefooghe is a leading exponent of this discipline and here he explains how it works.

Professionally, the so-called 'talking cure' has been the topic of my studies, my research and my practice for the last two decades. Ever since one of Freud's first patients - Anna O - coined the term, talking has seen to be the medium through which connections are made, unconscious desires uncovered, and trauma resolved. For psychoanalysts, psychologists and psychotherapists, language has been the currency through which you enter someone else's world. Just as the archaeologist painstakingly removes layers of dust before revealing some priceless find, so does the analyst chip away at the elaborate linguistic codes through which we construct our worlds. After all, language is perhaps the most intricate and sophisticated artefact we have. It's good to talk. It lets others in. It helps them understand you. Being listened to is powerful. Speaking releases. But what if you don't want to, or can't, talk?

Junior is 11 and has no language. He is diagnosed on the autistic spectrum. Holding his arm across his face most of the time, he does not invite people in. Charlene is well versed in the language of addiction. She comes out with all the sound-bites. But it all sounds empty. She is quite lost. Why, she mutters, does she still drink even though she very clearly knows what not to do? Billy mainly talks in expletives. Having been expelled for bullying from all schools locally, he is being looked after at the local Pupil Referral Unit. Suzanne, who has just received a five year sentence for grievous bodily harm with intent, doesn't trust anyone and is certainly not going to 'spill the beans' for some shrink. These four people are typical examples of those we work with. As you can see, sitting down in a consulting room and waiting for a conversation to develop may not be the most productive approach.

Enter the horses. It's very hard not to connect when you are asked to spend time with these amazing beasts. It is equally hard not to have an emotional reaction, even if this is initially in the form of fear. How people connect teaches us a lot about their internal worlds. Observing them as part of a herd is an extraordinary diagnostic tool. In its most basic conception, observing the horses interact with patients or participants functions as the methodology through which the therapist can connect where hitherto language had played that role.

Once a connection is established, a big piece of the work has been done. Junior's parents and carers could see that he was actually quite good at social communication, something people diagnosed on the spectrum are deemed to lack – they simply hadn't looked at Junior in that way. By introducing the rule in therapy that everyone should remain silent, language looses its significance momentarily. Other orders of communication can take centre stage.

Charlene starts to experience that the horses are mirrors. "They're not interested in me, there only interested in the grass that is just out of reach" were her first words when she started treatment. Now she has insight and notices when she is talking about herself rather than others, and can gain deeper understanding.

And Billy? Well, it is difficult to bully a horse that weighs over a tonne. Billy experienced firm boundaries being held, even if he did his damnedest to break them down. He learned that cooperation is less effort, it gives you results, and you actually feel good about yourself.

Suzanne, finally, can let go. In one of the first sessions, a horse stepped on her foot. Her tears weren't just about the immediate discomfort – Suzanne described how she suddenly realised she had been trodden on all her life. She needed to do things differently.

Would Junior, Charlene, Billy and Suzanne have achieved similar results without horses in therapy? They might. Yet my hunch is it would have been much slower, and much more difficult to reach such deep-seated issues in a very short time. The horses as co-therapists functioned as the technology through which people can connect with their emotions, just as language usually allows us to. None of them wanted, or could, talk. Once they had spent some time with our horses, there was no stopping their talk, or their communications.

The Last Herd

The Tourist Trade-3,
The Hampton Court Charabanc

Hampton Court, a Charabanc fit for a Palace

Queen Victoria opened Hampton Court Palace's gardens to the public in 1838 and visitors flocked to the gardens to experience the Maze, the Great Vine and the formal gardens. Horse-drawn charabancs would have been a common sight during the Victorian period, bringing visitors to the palace.

2017 saw the introduction of the new charabanc, the Tudor Rose, and visitors can tour the gardens in Victorian style. The vehicle is based on surviving historic vehicles as well as many old photographs and other images that survive. The result is a "Charabanc fit for a palace" but with an eye to modern needs. It's as close as possible to a Victorian horse-drawn charabanc but with a special 21st-century feature - unlike its Victorian predecessors, it is wheelchair accessible via a portable lift, as demonstrated by friend of Operation Centaur, Joe Gadd.

The Operation Centaur team brought Roy and Aragon to pull the inaugural ride and the The Reverend Anthony Howe, Chaplin from the Palace's Chapel Royal, blessed the vehicle and the horses.

Capability Brown 300 at Kew Gardens

Capability Brown 300, Kew Gardens

To mark the 300th anniversary of the birth of Capability Brown, Kew Gardens put on a pageant with the oldest surviving tree transplanter in the world. Tom and Heath were in action under the care of Edward MacDowell and Tom Nixon.

With the help of the Operation Centaur team, a Capability Brown actor, bell crier and costumed actors, visitors were transported back to the Georgian period to discover Capability Brown's revolutionary gardening techniques. Who needs a TARDIS when you have Shire horses to evoke times gone by?

Using the tree transporter, visitors saw a tulip tree moved for planting in an authentic reproduction of the way the great man would have planted trees.

100

The Last Herd

The Kensington Palace - Another Day, Another Great Urban Meadow

Harvesting at Kensington Palace

Another day, another urban meadow, this one in the grounds of Kensington Palace. The wildflowers not only attract tourists, but a varied collection of wildlife, which probably would not be seen in central London.

All these meadows need to be harvested to promote new growth, so Tom (the human) and Edward with the help of Michael Hynes, took Tom (the equine one that is) and Heath to Kensington Palace in a horse box. Once there, the team quickly attached the Shires to the hay cutter and took them round to the meadow.

Viewed from any direction it's hard to believe this is in central London, just a stone's throw away from the Royal Albert Hall and the almost manicured Hyde Park. Looking towards the palace, one would think it was the grounds of a great country house and in the other direction, you could be on wild heathland, a tribute to those who planned the meadow and brought a piece of wild country into the city.

Pictures - Page 106 - getting the Shires out of the horse box, by the Orangery. Page 107 - Mowing begins in the shadow of the palace.

Page 108 - Bringing the horses to the meadow and cutting proceeds. Page 109 - Michael Hynes looks on as Tom and Edward drive the Shires - hard to believe this is not a country farm.

The Last Herd

Hurst Park - Meeting The Community

Hurst Park - the Shires meet the local community.

Hurst Park Racecourse was a racecourse at Moulsey Hurst, West Molesey, Surrey. It was first laid out in 1890 and closed in 1962. The Triumph Hurdle was run here from 1939 until the course closed. It has now been transformed into a park by Thames Landscape Strategy and at this event, the local community came to meet the Shires, who are helping to manage the area.

Ham House Meadow

Ham House - Harvesting the Meadow

The Shires have a great role to play in the management of wildflower and wilderness areas. The meadow between Ham House and the River Thames at Ham is one such area and Operation Centaur's team are well up to the task. Tom and Edward with Linda Duffield and other volunteers and, of course, a couple of Shires, Tom and Heath, cut, raked and moved the hay from the meadow.

Using the reciprocating hay cutter, the newly acquired side delivery rake (a horse powered harvester without the cutter) plus old fashioned pitchforks and a low loader, the meadow was harvested and the resulting hay taken off to be stacked at the Shires base at the old stables in Home Farm, in Hampton Court, to provide winter feed and bedding.

Pictures -

Page 116/117 - Cutting the hay in Ham Meadow.

Page 118/119/120 - Cutting, raking and harvesting.

Winter Work - Harrowing and Logging

Winter Work, Harrowing Logging and some Christmas Rides.

The winter comes and our year's season with the Shires is fast coming to an end. But there is still a lot of work for "The Last Herd". Andy Moody and Tom Nixon worked with Nobby and Heath to scarify old pasture to promote growth. This was done at Kingston Fields at Hampton Court's Home Farm. They then did some logging there with Nobby. Tom took the opportunity to get some of the Shires working three in hand. Heath, Nobby and Tom took to this really well and Tom and Edward took them to Ham House meadow to chain harrow the meadow.

Pictures -

Top - Andy Moody logging in Kingston Fields with Nobby.

Below - Heath and Nobby on a winter's day at Home Farm.

Page 123 - Andy Moody logging in Kingston Fields with Nobby.

Page 124 - Tom Nixon with Nobby, Heath and Tom working three up in Kingston Fields.

Page 125 - Nobby and Heath in the diamond hard winter light on Home Farm as they scarify old pasture to promote next years growth.

124

Left - In Richmond Park, Tom adjusts the log arch to reduce friction to help the horses move logs more easily.

Above - Roy and Aragon, driven by Tom, take winter visitors round the park.

Right - On a misty day by the Thames in the meadow near Ham House, Tom Nixon has Murdoch, Heath and Tom three up, chain harrowing the wildflower meadow.

Page 128 - As winter turns back to spring, Tom Nixon is logging with Murdoch in Richmond Park.

The Human Staff

Dr Andreas Liefooghe – Co-Founder and Director

My relationship with horses goes back as far as I can remember. I was born in a small village in rural Flanders in the sixties, and horses were very much part of the scene. They weren't in their heyday but there were still horses around, horses that worked the land mainly. Not many horses were kept for leisure. One of my earliest memories is hearing the little bells of the heavy horses. They would have been Ardennes or Brabant horses just coming through the village, back from working the land. I was fascinated by horses. When I started riding, I pretty much did all the equestrian disciplines. I have always been very acutely aware of the relationships that you build with horses.

Operation Centaur as a term and as a concept has been in my mind for a very long time. I wanted to have something that looked at that intricate relationship between humans and horses. The image of a Centaur was central to that. I wanted something dynamic, which is where Operation comes from - dynamic and moving forward. In essence, we have four main areas of activity: conservation, heritage, community and therapy.

Our conservation work spans work in and around The Royal Parks and Historic Royal Palaces. Far from being a romanticised notion of using horses in a nostalgic way, we demonstrate that we can do a sensitive job efficiently and by threading lightly. The footprint of a Shire horse is far preferable than the tyre mark of a piece of heavy machinery. In effect, with our horses we have returned to

stewardship of the land. We do what needs to be done at the right time, working with nature – rather than working to a fixed schedule which is what most contractors do.

Evidence has shown so far that more wildflowers flourish where the grass is cut using Shires, and more variety of flowers too. In Richmond Park, we often leave a piece of bracken untouched because we spotted birds nesting. You can't see that from a noisy tractor cab! Adam Curtis, the Park Manager in Richmond, has done a tremendous job in keeping the Shires working to this effect.

In terms of heritage, we have been providing horses and carriages to Hampton Court Palace for the past 25 years. The last ten years involved working with Shires. We contacted Mr Gough, the Estates Manager of Hampton Court Palace, and a great champion of horses – in particular in relation to the incredible history horses have at Hampton Court.   He loved the idea of bringing Shire horses to the Palace. Of course, the obvious link with Hampton Court and Henry VIII is crucial - in many ways he was the founder of the breed. In my mind, the Shire is to Hampton Court as the raven is to the Tower.

"In my mind, the Shire is to Hampton Court as the raven is to the Tower".

When we decided on Shires, many people advised us to opt for *Percherons* or *Comtois*, or any other French breeds. Shire horses are rarer than Giant Pandas, so it is more difficult to find the right ones. And because the French eat their horses, their horse populations are actually a lot healthier and diverse than ours here in Britain. But we were very adamant that we wanted to have Shire Horses. Apart from the connection with Hampton Court, there is something so quintessentially British about them, some incredible nobility.   Our herd grew from the two original Shire horses who are now long passed away, to the herd of eight amazing horses that we have now. The last herd of working Shires in London.

It is not only the breed that we are helping to preserve by keeping them in the spotlight. It is also the many skills involved in working with horses in carriages, and on the land. These days, people would have to go to an agricultural show to observe this on a small scale. We do this work right in the heart of our capital city, and

people are simply in awe when they observe our team working. We have a strong group of volunteers, too, whom we teach horsemanship skills. Volunteers are vital for our work. It brings a sense of community, gives people a stake in their environment. It also means that we can get the work done quicker. With the right dose of people power added to our real horse power, we can compete with any tractor. We are living history, yet incredibly in tune with contemporary conservation needs.

I don't think we'll go back to the days where Shire Horses were ubiquitous and were used for transport. Yet if we are going to use these horses for other means, what else can we use them for? A more recent idea of ourse has been to deploy the retired Shires as therapy horses and to deliver equine assistance psychotherapy. It's amazing to work with them. Pretty much any horse you can do therapy with but the special thing about the Shire Horses is their size and the fact that they are - you know - we have used them in anti bullying programmes quite a lot - you can't bully a Shire Horse, they are too big, you have to work with them. You can't tell them what to do, you have to work with them and I think their size really adds a dynamic to the therapy.

Making a difference – this is what Operation Centaur is all about.

Edward MacDowell – Co-Founder and Head Coachman

I have been with horses most of my life. My family had horses, I used to go to work with my uncle's working horses and when I was a kid, the first horse I had was when I was 8, a pony called Kelly. From then on, I've always been with them in one form or another. I decided I wanted to become a farrier, so I went to Newmarket and took an apprenticeship there and became a registered farrier. The first horse I shod was in 1970 which was a race horse called Brigadier Gerard and he was in stud at that time, retired. I have been shoeing our horses ever since.

In the early 1980s, I started working with horses in the West End of London, driving carriage horses around Leicester Square at night and doing tourist rides. I stopped doing that when I got a call from Hampton Court Palace to provide carriage rides for Palace visitors. I have been working there now for over 25 years, and the last ten years with Shires. I had only worked with carriage horses up till then and I didn't really think I'd get on with Shires, they are all a bit big and lumpy and I thought they were a bit slow.

I fell in love with them from the word go, they were just great to work with. I don't know how to explain it but

they are more like colleagues rather than something you work with. With a Shire, you work with them because they are very big and if you upset them and put them in a bad mood, they'll stay in that mood all day and so you have got to keep on the right side of them. You work with them with a lot of respect and they are very powerful and they are very clever.

I love my job with Shire horses. I'm 63 and I have been with horses most of my life and every day I go to work, I learn something - they teach you something. They are amazing animals to work with. I like to communicate the joy they give me to other people. Nowadays, many people see animals as something apart from them, they never meet them nor do they get a chance to work with them. It's sad.   I think the Shire horse has a

"I don't know how to explain it but they are more like colleagues rather than something you work with"

place in the English soul. People of a certain age, all our grannies had little china Shire horses in their houses, brasses on their walls and things like that and it's like an idyllic idea of England that probably never was but anyway, we've all got it. That's how people react to Shires, it touches something deep in their soul really and even people who aren't English, they look on it as a very British thing, the Shire horse.

Most Americans are into Clydesdales which are the Scottish version but even so, they have that thing about them that it's a reminder of an idyllic past really and most people love them. There's not a lot of difference between a Shire and a Clydesdale. In the old days you could tell them very much apart. The Clydesdale is an older breed, it is Scottish and it came, as most of the big horses did, from Europe, from France I think, but the Scots always got on with everyone you see, so they were given these really good - by the French - they gave them big working horses. The English had to go and steal ours cos nobody liked us so, you know, they wouldn't give us, cos you've got to remember back in those days, they were war horses so they were looked upon as in the way we look on atom bombs or something. They were really machines that everyone wanted for war, so we weren't allowed them so we had to go and steal them from the Scots and the French and various others, the Flemish, big Flemish horses we got over in the 16th century and from that, we bred our own horses. Now the Scottish horse is usually a bit taller and a bit rangier. The English Shire horse is much more compact and much more - they always remind me of a doorman or a bouncer, they've usually got the old Roman nose you see, they are quite thick set and yeah, very stoical horses they are. I love them.

There has to be a place for a working horse, and funnily enough, I think there's more place for the working horse in an urban environment, in the parks and in flower meadows and woodlands that exist inside London and other urban areas. We can't compete in the countryside with combine harvesters and tractors and huge fields. We come into our own in smaller areas where we do less damage to the environment. Slowly but surely we're carving a niche for the Shire in the cities. People are starting to ride them now, but they're not really cut out for that – it's like taking a tractor for a spin down the M1. No, the Shire is a working horse and we seem to have found a space for them to thrive.

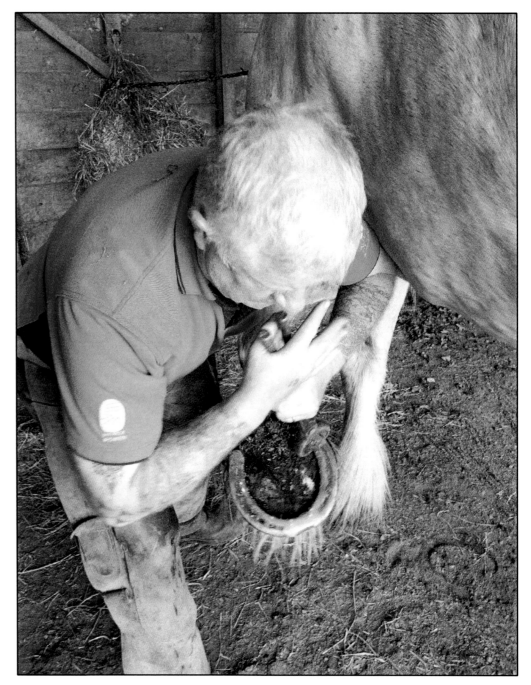

Tom Nixon – Head Horseman

My first experience of heavy farm horses was as a child of about 5 walking between the handles of a plough as my father opened drills for potatoes on a South County, Dublin, farm where he was the farm manager. There was no tractor on this mixed dairy and tillage farm so what could not be done with the old farm horse, contractors were hired to do. Because of ill health he had to retire early and at 14 years old I left school and took over from him. I bought my first workhorse when I was 15 and a second the following year. Now I had a pair to plough with and carry out all the jobs that a small tractor could do on a farm. I learnt my trade from my father who was an old fashioned horseman and in my mind the greatest horseman I have ever known.

In 1993 I left the farm in Dublin and went south to Killarney and the Muckross traditional farms where I brought 4 of my own Shire horses and large array of carts and equipment to take up a new position as horseman on this newly developed tourist farm where only horse power was used to recreate farm life in the 20s and 30s. After three years I moved on and bringing with me a pair of Shires and Brewer's Dray I began doing promotional and film work also attending many shows and festivals around the country. Trojan Heavy Horses was the only commercial working Shire horses in Ireland and soon the work led us into the forestry sector where private land owners and sawmills would employ us to extract valuable timber from difficult sites where machinery was either not wanted or could not get to.

In 2015, I came across a job advertised on from a company in London called Operation Centaur. They were looking for an experienced horseman to work with their Shires and so I answered the advert. Two weeks later I had an interview and after being offered the position, my partner Tracy and I decided that this was an opportunity too good to pass up so I'm still here working with Operation Centaur, mainly with the Shires but also with the six grey carriage horses used with the Landau.

Our eight Shires are used to perform many jobs but we specialise in conservation and heritage work mainly in The Royal Parks and Historic Royal Palaces. Being the only working herd of Shires in the London area, it is of

"To me there is nothing to compare to working with these magnificent animals"

the utmost importance that we continue to bring these beautiful horses out and show young and old alike that they still hold a valuable place in our history and even more so in our future. Looking back at my life, the common denominator in everything I have done has been with heavy horses. A life where many times there have been more paydays than pay cheques. A life that has caused more than a man's fair share of wear and tear on the body, like walking 11 miles to plough one acre in the day or stumbling up and down the side of a mountain, day in day out, snagging timber, usually in unforgiving rain and wind.

But this the life I have chosen and a life I would choose again if given the chance. To me, there is nothing to compare to working with these magnificent animals, to stand between a pair of 18hh Shires after a days work and smell the sweat that they have worked up in their toil to please the man working with them, to hear and see their excitement when you come into the stable yard on a dark winters' morn to give them their breakfast, and to stand amongst them in a field and watch them jostling each other for your attention. This is something very special and will never be experienced from a tractor.

I always say when you're going home from work in the evening and looking forward to going back to work the following morning, well, then you have been right and very lucky in your choice of jobs.

142

Andrew Moody - Horseman.

I first started working with horses 22 years ago when I was 11 years old. My mum got me into it, she used to ride as a little girl and she told me that when I was little, my first word that I spoke was 'horse'. So perhaps it was pre-destined that my life was going to be with horses. I studied animal behaviourism at university, so I had a strong focus on horsemanship, and horse relationships.

In 2006, I got a job at the Royal Mews as a Livery person. My role was to care for the Queen's carriage horses, and I was trained in ceremonial carriage driving. I started by being a footman, then an outrider, riding the horses in front of the carriages. I then progressed to driving pairs of horses and riding postilion, which is when you ride the horses when they are pulling the carriages. Once you master this, you move to learning to drive four in hand coachwork. I had a role in starting to train young horses in harness as well.

I started work with Operation Centaur in 2012, so at that time, the conservation work with the Royal Parks has just started. My role was quite varied. I started with mowing grass and rolling bracken. I then moved on to help with Equine Assisted Psychotherapy, as that is a real interest

of Andreas's, he's been researching and working on that for many years. When I came on board there was an opportunity to pilot a range of new programmes.

It's amazing to work with Shires. They have a particular pace that they work at and particularly if you are working with them on conservation work or working on the land, mowing the grass or back in the woodlands. When you are working at their pace, you connect into their rhythm, which is more in harmony with nature. So when you are working with the rhythm of the Shires, you are also working with the rhythm of the nature round you and you just start to notice things around you that you wouldn't notice if you were working with machinery - the birds, the flowers and the dragonflies and whatever else there is around you. So for me that is a really important experience.

"When you are working with the rhythm of the Shire horses, you are also working with the rhythm of the nature round you"

A working relationship with a Shire horse is quite a special bond, which takes time and develops over the years that you work with them. You get to know them very well and they get to know you. The working breeds, breeds that have worked with people for a long time, there is something in them that seeks to work with you so when you find that you can work with them in that way, there is something quite special about that. They are very special horses.

Henry Coward – Horseman.

I started working with horses in 1974 at Young and Co's Brewery. I worked inside the brewery to start with and then a job became available after about 12 months on the horses and I applied and I worked there till I left in 2007, so I was just over 32 years working. I started in the stables as the boy for a little while, a few months, and then you'd go out on the road with a senior person and another one to make three of you go and then you'd go and see how everything went on and then eventually, after about 18 months, I was allowed to drive. Then I carried on driving for the rest of my time there, on deliveries mainly. My main job was delivering beer through the week.

When I first started, we had a delivery side and a show side, and we must have had about 22 horses between the show side and the work side. On the work side 4 pair went out every day and they done a three mile radius of the brewery delivering to all the Young's pubs. They take on average about two and a half ton of beer per load. Our maximum weight for our deliveries was three ton. We'd go from Wandsworth, which is the central place, to Tooting which was the furthest, then to Chelsea, and then we would go to Barnes and the other way, we'd go to Wimbledon Common.

We'd also go to all the local fairs, country shows. The main ones were like the East of England, the Royal, all the big ones. We'd do Horse of the Year Show and some of our work also was doing carnivals and fetes of a weekend for local charities which was a high percent of work for about ten or twelve weeks during the summer. We used to be out every Saturday and Sunday, basically, doing something. It's a great shame Young's got rid of their horses. It was a sign of the times really, the brewery decided they wanted to move from Wandsworth and it wouldn't have been feasible to have horses that are from outside London, so that is why they stopped delivering beer in September 2006.

"After about 18 months, I was allowed to drive. Then I carried on driving for the rest of my time there"

I started working with Operation Centaur in the stables in Hampton Court in about 2009 and I have worked between the stables and have just recently started here (Holly Lodge in Richmond Park) as well. I have been the longest serving member, other than the governors here. I prefer driving the Charabanc, you are high up, nice and high up. You can see more when you are up high and you can see more of what you actually explain as you go round.

We get the odd person who says the horses should be out in the field doing nothing, but the Shire horse is bred to work. If they don't work they might as well not exist really. They are happier when they are working. You can tell that because when you go in the morning, you can tell if they are up for the day's work - it's like people. If you are up for the day's work, you'll go and you're happy. You look at the horse and say, yes, he is up for it. You get them ready and you go in and they do their work.

Tanya Melton - Coachman

None of my family is into horses, my mum was actually terrified of them. I grew up with livery stables down my road, so we used to have horses go past the house every day. I used to sit and watch them and I just loved them. And then one day, I was out walking my dog, I must have been about ten years old and a woman drove past with a pair of Shetland ponies. It was just the dearest little thing I had ever seen in my life, it was amazing. So I followed her home to her stables and I asked her if I could help, basically just convinced her to let me stay and she let me. I washed out buckets and got to brush the ponies and I thought it was brilliant, absolutely fantastic. Then we took the ponies to the field, and being Shetlands, one of them pulled the rope out of my hands, spun round and kicked me. I had to go home with this great big bruise on my leg and it was like "What's happened to you?" and I said "Well, I've met this woman with Shetlands and I got kicked, but she said I could go back next weekend if that's OK" - and that was it, really.

Maureen started teaching me about looking after her Shetlands and taught me to drive. I used to drive them as singles and we went up to Windsor Park Equestrian Club, up in the Great Park and we'd do dressage and combined driving and competition driving, like the Duke of Edinburgh.

He used to see us quite a lot and we'd park next to him with the Shetlands and he'd be with a team of Fells and just laugh at us because we had such tiny little things. Maureen is now 79 and just bought a new pair of youngsters to drive, but she still has one of the Shetlands I started with who is now well into his 30s. He gave my son Tomas his first carriage driving lesson.

My parents wanted me to go to university to study English and I went to have a look at a couple of universities. I didn't feel ready for further study, and decided to work with John Sear who worked in Windsor as a horse-drawn taxi man. He had the last Hackney licence, and he did tours up and down the Long Walk. He gave me a job driving weddings at 18. We also helped with the Lord Mayor's Parade. We took a pair to the Royal Mews at Buckingham palace where we would put them to the Balmoral Sociable (a favourite carriage of Queen Victoria and was also used for Queen Elizabeth's grandson Peter Philips' wedding at Windsor). Heading through London with a dozen other carriages was pretty special.

"Then I told my parents I was finally ready to go uni, but I wasn't going to do English any more, I was going to study horses"

When I was finally ready for university, I decided to read Equine Studies at Writtle College. This included science, anatomy, physiology, dissecting horses, learning about how everything worked. We learned how to run a business, run events involved in the horse industry. We also had young stock work, so I did stud modules about breeding horses, young stock work, and training young horses.   During that time, I was also a back-stepper - the person who stands on the back of the carriage in combined driving. I had a friend who used to go and do the nationals in Essex, so I back-stepped for him in different events.

Whilst I was at university, I took a gap year and went to America. I lived at Ayrshire Farm in Upperville, Virginia which is owned by Sandy Lerner, who was the co-founder of Cisco Systems.   The Farm had rare English breeds, including pigs, cattle and Shire horses.   At the time I was there, she had 50 Shire horses, including two stallions, new-borns and retired horses. We did everything. We bred them, we showed them, we rode

them, we drove them. Sandy had a coach that we put a four in hand of Shire horses to, and we went all around the different shows and coaching rallies. I worked under Paul May, who was a British showing driver who had been trained by Cynthia Haydon, who is one of the big names in showing driving. She was formidable, so it was quite an education.

I came back, I finished my degree and I needed a job but there are not a lot of driving jobs going. Driving yards want people who can be grooms and work up because they have got their drivers. I learned to ride, and instead worked in polo. I worked in Cirencester for a couple of seasons and then moved to Windlesham at Ascot Park, where I ran lessons and tournaments and organised chukkas. I had my son and had to stop doing so much riding, so I went back to driving with John. It was brilliant because Tomas as a baby could come with me and he'd just sleep in the back of the carriage whilst I took them out driving, it was a great way to make sure he got his afternoon nap! I really needed to find something a bit more permanent.

That's when I found Operation Centaur.

Linda Duffield - Volunteer

I'm a retired diplomat, I've spent 27 years working in the Foreign and Commonwealth Office in a variety of jobs around the world including as British High Commissioner to Sri Lanka and the Maldives, and as Ambassador to the Czech Republic. I retired three years ago and moved back to Richmond and was looking to get more involved in local projects. I started to volunteer as a gardener at Ham House, a National Trust property locally and through them, they asked me to manage their teams of volunteers who were going to be involved in a new project with Thames Landscape Strategy and Operation Centaur. I went to meet both organisations and have been volunteering ever since with both of them.

I love working with the Shire horses. I think the heavy horses and the Shires as a breed are very steady, very intelligent animals and very good to be around. So in all the jobs I have done with the Shires, I feel very comfortable. They have a different nature to other horses.

It is quite heavy work but I am enjoying doing outdoors work. I am interested in land management. I was very attracted by the idea of managing the land in a more natural way, not using heavy machinery that impacts on the land. That is part of the reason why I work with the National Trust, with Operation Centaur and Thames Landscape Strategy. So the idea of using horses to do the work that we have become used to seeing machinery do is quite appealing. It is heavy work for those who are managing the horses and for those who are

volunteering around them, but it is also a great way to get fit and keep fit in retirement. All the jobs are completely different. I have worked on the heritage rides, taking charabanc tours around the gardens at Hampton Court Palace. I enjoy garden history so giving those tours is interesting, but it's the quiet periods, getting the horses ready, walking them through Home Park in the mornings which is just magical. When there is nobody around, just the deer and you feel 'am I this close to Central London and I'm in a natural environment with horses and deer?'. That's lovely.

I have enjoyed supporting Operation Centaur with their fundraising winter rides in Richmond Park. I have probably spent most time working with the Shires in the Avenues around Ham, linking Ham House and its history with the wider land management of the estates around the property, and I have enjoyed working with volunteers and helping them understand what the horses do. It's a great attraction, not only for those who are working around the horses, but also for visitors, members of the public, local people, who are all interested in why we are working with horses and I enjoy talking to them about the horses.

I also enjoy volunteering with the therapy work that Operation Centaur use the Shires for. I'm supporting them with their work with young children, children in foster care through "Achieving for Children", and also their therapy work in prisons, working with recovering addicts. It's really interesting to see how people respond to Shire horses. They are big, people are often quite nervous around them to start with, but they soon get a real respect for the horses. The sheer size but also the quietness of the horses not only has a calming effect, but it helps people reflect on themselves and their behaviour. I can see how effective they are in therapy programmes.

I'd never been around horses, so I have come very late in life to horses and I have learned a lot from the Operation Centaur team. I read a little bit around the subject but mostly learning by observation and from people who have been working with them for many years. I am having some lessons in driving the horses. I want to be able to do more. I am very happy also helping to muck out and do all the other necessary work that goes with horses, I think that goes as part of the package.

The human staff and volunteers, without whom none of the events would be possible, pose with Nobby and Murdoch at a logging and forestry demonstration in Richmond Park.

The Equine Staff

Stable name: Nobby
Registration name: Chelsworth Nobby
Age: 7 years

Stable name: Tom
Registration name: Springbank Tom
Age: 8 years

Stable name: Heath
Registration name: Heathfield Forester
Age: 10 years

Stable name: Joey
Registration name: Forest Nicodemus
Age: 7 years

164

Stable name: Massey
Registration name: Massey
Age: 12 years

Stable name: Murdoch
Registration name: Murdoch The Flying Scotsman
Age: 10 years

Stable name: Roy

Registration name: Royale II

Age: 20 years

Stable name: Aragon

Registration name: Rambo

Age: 18 years

166

Paul Stewart is an award winning photojournalist and press photographer who has worked around the world for national papers, agencies and magazines. He also undertakes work for charities, using photography to raise awareness of social issues. He currently combines working as Night Picture Editor of the Daily Express and shooting personal projects, such as this book. For more information about him and his work please visit:-

paulstewartphoto.co.uk

The Last Herd

Photography into ART

ISBN 978-0-9957092-1-8   £34.99